OVERWHELMED
NO MORE!

Love Yourself to Wealth

Janna Chin

BALBOA.
PRESS

A DIVISION OF HAY HOUSE

Balboa Press books may be ordered through booksellers or by contacting:

Balboa Press
A Division of Hay House
1663 Liberty Drive
Bloomington, IN 47403
www.balboapress.com
1 (877) 407-4847

Because of the dynamic nature of the Internet, any web addresses or links contained in this book may have changed since publication and may no longer be valid. The views expressed in this work are solely those of the author and do not necessarily reflect the views of the publisher, and the publisher hereby disclaims any responsibility for them.

The author of this book does not dispense medical advice or prescribe the use of any technique as a form of treatment for physical, emotional, or medical problems without the advice of a physician, either directly or indirectly. The intent of the author is only to offer information of a general nature to help you in your quest for emotional and spiritual well-being. In the event you use any of the information in this book for yourself, which is your constitutional right, the author and the publisher assume no responsibility for your actions.

Any people depicted in stock imagery provided by Thinkstock are models, and such images are being used for illustrative purposes only. Certain stock imagery © Thinkstock.

Print information available on the last page.

ISBN: 978-1-5043-5876-7 (sc)
ISBN: 978-1-5043-5877-4 (hc)
ISBN: 978-1-5043-5875-0 (e)

Library of Congress Control Number: 2016909045

Balboa Press rev. date: 07/22/2016

Contents

Money Business and Financial Abundance

Join the Overwhelmed *No More!* Love Yourself to Wealth Community Today

This book is only the beginning of your love affair with yourself, your life and your business. There's a lot more tools, resources, and connection at www.Janna-Chin.com.

Ongoing support and community are essential for success in any area of your life. One of the biggest factors in my wellness and success has been being part of a community of like-minded women where we guide each other, hold each other accountable, cheer for each other, love one another and grow together. I want this for you, too.

I've put together more tools, resources, education, programs, tools, and ongoing support for you. Join me at www.Janna-Chin.com to learn how you can:

1. **Join our exclusive online community.** Connect with other women entrepreneurs, change makers and leaders reading the book who are experiencing transformation and results. Ask questions, share insights and grow together.

2. **Start an Overwhelmed *No More!* Women's Circle or Meetup.** Download a free guide to starting your own local or virtual community to take the Overwhelmed *No More!* Love Yourself to Wealth journey with.

3. **Do the exercises.** Download the PDFs and print out all the exercises and worksheets from the book.

4. **Access exclusive webinars, programs and recommendations.** As I have fresh insights and new material, I'll be sure to share them with you on the website.

5. **Share your success.** Share your own story of falling in love with yourself, your life and your business. Read the success stories of other women to keep you inspired.

Visit www.Janna-Chin.com to join the women's community and go deeper with the book.

Loving Yourself First

Loving Yourself First

Loving myself first.
I'm afraid it would mean, I'm no longer willing to be a martyr.

It's a disgrace to barter myself for love.
I can't be for them what I need to be for me.
It's a travesty to be taking time for me when I have all these responsibilities.
So many people count on me. They need me, don't you see?

I don't want to let them down.
I can't bear to see them frown.

This is the turmoil women go through. Not knowing where they end and others begin.

The notions and expectations of who and what we should be, weigh heavily on our hearts. A constant conflict that lies within. We battle within ourselves, guilt, shame, despair, being overwhelmed and fatigued. Feeling inadequate and not measuring up. Wanting to prove to ourselves and the world, we can do and have it all. Giving and giving until we are no more of who we were. Losing ourselves in a sea of being overwhelmed. We can no longer see who we were meant to be. Somewhere in our confusion, we know deep down that it starts at home in our hearts- the place where all love starts. We've been searching and longing for love that has always been within us all along.

You *can* heal your heart.

It begins with you...

Introduction

I'm known as the 'Burnout Slayer' and 'Profit Accelerator.' As a successful coach of entrepreneurs, I assist women to powerfully break-free from being overwhelmed and into their greatest financial abundance.

I've worked with women entrepreneurs from all over the country who share with me their stories of turmoil-they don't know where they end and others begin. Over the past fifteen years, I've developed powerful tools and processes that are so life changing and transforming that I've often quickly worked myself out of a job. I'm excited to share some of these powerful tools with you, several of which will be in the following pages of this book.

I have the great honor of working with extraordinary women. Women who passionately believe in making a difference and contributing to the world in a big way to make it a better place. Women who juggle many roles and responsibilities and take care of the world with grace, yet somehow have forgotten how to adore and cherish themselves. We are all beautiful, magnificent women who deserve to be loved and adored, and prioritized first. This book is written as a guide and resource for you to find your way back to yourself- a tool for exploring your own answers for inner transformation, self-love, and freedom. My biggest hope is for you to use this book as a resource and guide to create your most outrageously wonderful, beyond joyous, and abundantly, prosperous life!

Unlocking the Mystery of Women Being Overwhelmed *No More!*

Unlocking the key to being overwhelmed no more has until now, been a mystery. You may have found yourself looking and desperately seeking answers to escape the overwhelm of your everyday reality. What you may not have known is that you have always had the keys to unlock this mystery within you already.

Overwhelmed *No More!* Love Yourself to Wealth is an empowering guide brimming with inspirational poetry, exercises, worksheets, power affirmations and conversation starters you can use to find your own answers and blaze your own trail towards healing, peace, and prosperity.

How to Get the Most From This Book

Inspirational Poems, Heart Questions, Exercises, and Worksheets

In order to create lasting change, I've discovered women must go deep within themselves to unlock the answers they're seeking to create profound change and transformation. All the poems take you through a process of self-evaluation and introspection. The worksheets and heart questions assist you with discovering powerful insights into what may be underlying your personal circumstances and provides you with guidelines to create tools and step-by-step action plans to make positive changes in your life and business.

Power Affirmations

The power affirmations are positive affirmations designed to awaken and empower your inner potential and enable you to manifest your highest intentions. To really manifest your intentions, say the power affirmations out loud in your own voice, and in a way that helps you to feel empowered. Meditate on your power affirmations in the morning, during the day when you need a boost, and in the evening before you sleep. Focus on the the meaning of each power affirmation and feel the feelings associated with the affirmation. Every time you say the power affirmation out loud, take a moment to really breathe in the feelings of each affirmation.

Conversation Starters

The conversation starters can be used in women's groups where women support each other and share their wisdom and experiences pertaining to topics all women can relate to. Poetry readings and women's groups using Overwhelmed *No More!* Love Yourself to Wealth can easily be facilitated by following the book's format. If you'd like to experience even deeper results, start an Overwhelmed *No More!* women's group and/or book club to create a sisterhood of support. Or, start a Meetup in your area using this book as a guide. By doing so, you would be "paying it forward," helping yourself deeply, and creating a community of support of like-minded women. Here you can experience heartfelt conversations, and true connection, without stress and feeling overwhelmed.

The Beginning of a
New Me

The Beginning of a New Me

Keeled over on the floor, I can still remember that day as if it were yesterday... It was the worst day of my life.

Keeled over in so much pain, my hand over my heart as it broke into a thousand pieces. It felt like knives stabbing me over and over, again and again, ripping my heart apart into a million pieces. I had never felt so much pain until that terrible day.

As I lay on the plush white carpet on the bathroom floor, holding my heart, hanging on for dear life, I felt my heart break open, bleeding all over the carpet. No one could have seen the blood stains on the plush white carpet, except me. It was my pain. My heartbreak. My misery.

Sobbing uncontrollably, I hurt so deeply. The pain I was in hit the core of all I was. All my wounds came from the rejection and heartbreak that up until that point, I thought was the love of my life.

I couldn't get out of bed for weeks. I didn't know how this could happen to me. I gave him everything. My heart. My soul. My everything was for him. It was all about him. I gave and gave until I lost sight of me. Not knowing who I was, I was totally empty.

Feeling like an empty, hollow, shell of a person, I had nothing more to give.

I had to learn how to pick up the pieces of what was left of me and start over...from scratch.

I had to learn how to be the person who loved me for me. I didn't know how to do that. All I knew how to do was help everyone else so that I could forget about me.

I finally hit rock bottom.

This was my moment of truth.

The definition of insanity is doing the same thing over and over and expecting different results. I was tired of the insanity. I could go back to who I used to be or I could learn to become a new me. The former was easy. The latter terrifying.

All I knew was, I couldn't keep going on the way I had been. I really had no choice. I had to choose me. I had to choose the path of finding a new me- a new and improved, better me.

All I wanted was to have healthy relationships. Somehow I found Codependents Anonymous (CODA), where the only requirement for membership is the desire for healthy relationships.

I knew I had a long road ahead to find a new me. At first I went to CODA meetings everyday for months, and everyday for months I cried and cried- realizing how I had mistreated myself as the last priority and compromised myself for other people's approval; desperately seeking, but always falling short of feeling loved.

I was looking for love in all the wrong places.

I never felt good enough so I sought to prove to myself and the world that I was good enough.

Deep down.

I really didn't believe it.

Being good enough is a feeling that we can only experience *within* ourselves. No one can give it to us. It's not something outside of ourselves. It's not external. It's internal. It's not something we experience by *doing.* No amount of acknowledgement, achievement, recognition, letters after our names, or honorary awards can magically make us feel good enough. It is something that must be felt in our hearts. It is something we must truly believe within the core of all that we are. I didn't know that growing up when I went to college and graduated with honors, earned my Master's degree in Counseling Psychology, or when I bought my first house at twenty-eight.

I was still trying to prove to the world, and mostly to myself, that I was good enough by *doing* for everyone else. I didn't know it at the time, but unconsciously, I thought that if I could just do enough service, give more of myself; my time, energy, dedication, and loyalty, I would have finally proven I was lovable and good enough.

Little did I know, I could never really know true love until I learned to wholeheartedly love myself first.

From the day I started attending CODA, I vowed I was going to change- never was I going to love someone so much that I would lose myself completely. No longer was I going to be my last priority. It was through divine intervention that I learned boundaries.

For once in my life, I learned that I could set limits on my time, my body, and my emotions, based on what felt right for me. I learned the magic word that somehow I had forgotten. The one word that magically protected me from emotional harm and time sucking vampires. The one magic word, "No," changed my life. I started using my voice- finding the courage to express my true feelings, instead of fearing rejection and being a people pleasing doormat just to be in the false illusion that I belonged and was good enough.

I learned to say "No" without feeling guilty or ashamed. I could feel my feelings and set limits when I felt uncomfortable; starting with all the chatter in my head. The never-ending self-critic that haunted me all my life- the voice that told me I wasn't good enough, to try harder, to strive for perfection because that's the only way I would ever be good enough and worthy of love, acceptance, and approval.

As I was working on becoming a new me, emotionally and spiritually, it was too late for my body. After years of working sixty to eighty hours a week as a psychotherapist, driving all over town, sucking up and absorbing all the pain and trauma of my client's experiences— taking care of everyone else and neglecting myself, my body finally broke down.

One day, I woke up and I just could not get out of bed. My body hurt all over. I could feel aches and pains in every crevice of my body. It felt like I had the flu: weak, achy all over, and so fatigued I couldn't even sit at the computer or have a five minute conversation without getting so exhausted I had to go back to bed and pass out. It was like I was ninety-five in a thirty something year old's body. After months of excruciating pain, I learned I had Fibromyalgia which was pretty much just a bunch of symptoms that doctors treated like a "phantom" make believe disease because there were no tests to prove the pain existed. There was nothing scientific to prove anything was wrong with me so of course, there were no treatments and barely any sympathy from doctors, friends, or family; they could hardly understand why I was incapacitated all the time, unable to work, and could barely function.

Looking back, that was the darkest time of my life. As a "go getter" and woman who was always doing and working towards goals, engaged in service and helping others, it was beyond depressing to be bedridden and rendered completely helpless. It would take months for me to gather up enough strength to leave the house or make it to doctor appointments or holistic, health-care treatments.

I always had trouble sleeping ever since I was a little girl. I would toss and turn all night. My mind would spin out of control, replaying scenarios in my head, changing and controlling outcomes in my imagination. I was living in anxiety, worry, and fear. During the day, I was too exhausted to function and at night, I lay awake an insomniac.

As I started to make progress to improve my health and self-care, I learned how to re-enter the world on healthy terms. Never again was I going to get to a place of overwhelm and exhaustion. Never again was I going to lay awake, worrying and in anxiety- a crazy in the head insomniac. I learned how to heal my problems using mind, body, and spiritual approaches based on self-love, health, well- being, peace, serenity, and a meaningful life filled with purpose.

Today, I get to work with extraordinary women. Women who passionately believe in making a difference and contributing to the world in a big way to make it a better place. Women who juggle many roles and responsibilities and take care of the world with grace, yet somehow have forgotten how to adore and cherish themselves. We are all beautiful, magnificent women who deserve to be loved and adored and prioritized first. This book is written as a guide and resource for you to find your way back to yourself- a tool for exploring your own answers for inner transformation, self-love, and freedom. My biggest hope is for you to use this book as a resource and guide to create your most outrageously wonderful, beyond joyous, and abundantly, prosperous life!

Getting to I'm Enough

"If you cannot find peace within yourself, you will never find it anywhere else." -Marvin Gaye

Getting to I'm Enough

How will we ever get to this place of "I'm enough?"
"I'm enough."
Just two simple words
If fully embraced could change the world…
How we feel about ourselves
What we do
Why we do it
At the very essence of "I'm enough" is complete love and
surrender to what is.
It's a love of ourselves that we in turn
can give to others.
There's no need for control or judgment.
There's simply complete self-acceptance and gratitude for
who we are.
No longer would we need to strive to prove our worthiness
for approval and acceptance.
We would not have to work endless hours
to achieve goals that in the end,
are meaningless and leave us with regret.
The energy we didn't put into making a difference
only to have a bunch of zeros in our bank accounts
that we can't take with us anyway.
It doesn't matter what we do

if we don't do it with heart
with love
with compassion
Starting with ourselves
That's where the difference begins
at home
in our hearts.
When you finally embrace
wholeheartedly with all that you are
"I'm enough,"
Fear will leave your side and
peace will find it's way.

Mary's Story

Before she came to me as a client, Mary had always made just enough to get by and sometimes would have less than twenty dollars to her name. Although she was incredibly talented and had been an entrepreneur with her own business for over twenty years, love, happiness, and success eluded her. She had been married to a man she constantly had to "save" and now that she was divorced, she was ready to really live, really love, and financially prosper.

In our first session, Mary explained in painstaking detail how she wanted more money, love, and self-worth, but she had underlying fears that kept her from really stepping into the life of prosperity she truly desired. Her biggest challenge was her prevailing belief that she didn't deserve to be happy and successful. During our work together, I supported Mary by helping her to discover and understand her pattern of self-sabotage. Then I provided her with empowering coaching sessions to help her break through her fear of success and failure and belief of not being good enough. Mary also received personalized tools to assist her with coping with her fears; this included tools to shift her negative, low self-worth mindset to a success mindset, which empowered her to finally feel good enough and fill her cup to the brim with self-love.

After just a few sessions, Mary overcame her fear of success and failure. She also overcame the belief that she wasn't good enough. This helped her to fully step into the life of prosperity she had always dreamed of. Today, she is a highly sought-after coach with a waiting list of clients lined up to work with her! Imagine how delighted I was to find out that a few months later, Mary was also enjoying beautiful bliss and deep connection with the love of her life and soul mate.

Heart Questions

When did you start feeling you weren't good enough?
What messages did your parents and authority figures convey to you, growing up to convince you that you weren't good enough?
Are you willing to let go of their opinions and projections of you?
How do you want to feel about yourself?
What are three things you can do to start feeling the way you want to feel?
Make a list of qualities and characteristics you value about yourself.
Make a list of qualities and characteristics people have valued and appreciated about you.
You can be loved, valued, included, and validated, without people pleasing or *doing* anything. How can you love yourself first simply just by *being* (you)?
Are you willing to commit to being good enough and setting yourself free from self-condemnation and judgment?

I'm Good Enough Vow

If you're ready to commit to yourself, stand up, place your hand on your heart and say the following pledge out loud:

"I, _____, vow to accept myself as a lovable and worthwhile person. I am enough. I am good enough. No longer am I going to buy into other people's projections of me. From now on, I'm going to love myself unconditionally and be my own best friend. I only need to do my best in everything I do. As long as I do my best, it will be good enough. Today, I'm breaking up with my inner critic. Her constant criticisms no longer serve me. And so it is and so it shall be."

Power Affirmations

I am enough.
I've always been enough.

 **Conversation Starters**

In what areas of your life do you feel you're not enough?

What can you do to start feeling good enough?

Do you want to finally feel good enough? Visit www.Janna-Chin.com/Good-Enough for more free tools.

Overwhelm

"Let whatever you do today be enough." -Anonymous

Overwhelm

So sneaky it can be.
You're just going along
with your routine and

Suddenly
Blam! You can't breathe.

Suffocated you can't see
Where it came from
Out of nowhere you can't breathe.

You're surprised it crept in
The never-ending To Do List
Even when you sleep.

Mother, leader, wife, trendsetter
you might be
Thinking, "I can do it all. You'll see."

Then one day, you're questioning, "Is it just me?"
Everyone else seems to be doing it so easily
What's wrong with me?

Guilt, shame, fatigue
It all comes up at once naturally.

So overwhelmed, you can't see what's in front of you.

The present moment is a distant memory
It's time to prepare for the future can't you see?

I have something to prove
I must show you that I'm worthy.

Or else I don't think anyone will love me.
I guess overwhelmed I'll just be.

Until the day I decide to love me for me.

Heart Questions

How do you get overwhelmed?
How do you put others first?
What can you do to take care of yourself first?
How you can you start loving and taking care of yourself first before everyone else?
What do you tell yourself to rationalize taking care of everyone else before your own wants and needs? List everything you tell yourself.
What are your needs and wants? Make a list of your wants and needs.
What three things can you start doing this week to start taking care of yourself and get your needs and wants met?

What three things will you do to start taking care of yourself first?

Emotionally:

Physically:

Spiritually:

What positive self-talk can you tell yourself to love yourself first? Write down three positive self-talk statements you will start using to start loving yourself first.

Repeat your positive self-talk statements every time you start to put others first before your own self-care.

Power Affirmations

Today I commit to taking care of me.
I am a loving and worthwhile person and I choose to feel joyous, prosperous, and free!

 **Conversation Starters**

How does overwhelm steal your joy?

What can you do to stay out of overwhelm and experience more work life balance and joy in your life?

Do you want to break-free from overwhelm and experience more ease and joy in your life and business? Visit www.Janna-Chin.com/ Break-Free to download more Free tools.

Showing Up for Yourself

"You yourself, as much as anybody else in the entire universe deserve your love and affection."-Buddha

Showing Up for Yourself

How do you sell yourself short
Cheat yourself of love and self-care?

Abandon your needs, wants, and desires
Sacrifice for other's sake.

Give and give
Until you feel you're going to break.

How did this happen to you?
When did you become a martyr?
And forget who you are.

What does it take to get this woman back...
To her essence and higher self?

When is she going to show up for herself?

Love Meditation

May I be peaceful, happy, and light in body and spirit.
May I be safe and free from injury.
May I be free from anger,
fear, and anxiety.
May I learn to look at myself with the eyes of
understanding and love.
May I be able to live fresh, solid, and free.
May I be free from attachment and aversion,
but not be indifferent.

-Thich Nhat Hanh

Heart Questions

If you were the best version of yourself, what would that look like?

Where has your love for yourself not yet reached?

How would you be treating yourself differently if you were madly in love with yourself? (Falling in love with yourself looks like how you treat the people you care most about.)

How would you "show up" differently?

Power Affirmations

Showing up for myself, I only give when it feels right in my heart.

Showing up for myself, I know who I am, what I want, and always speak my truth.

 **Conversation Starters**

Are there any areas in your life where you feel you may be overlooking your needs, wants, or desires?

How can you start showing up for yourself?

In-to-me-I-see

"Let yourself be deeply seen. Love with your whole heart even when there are no guarantees."-Brene Brown

In-to-me-I-see

Intimacy the capacity to love.
To share and care, showing parts of ourselves- to be really seen.
It's a feeling, a closeness with your Self and others in deep.

Intimacy is sharing the deepest parts of yourself without hiding who you are.
It's loving your Self.
Giving of yourself.
Your humanness.
Your hopes, dreams, pain, and sorrow.

In-to-me-I-see.
There are no walls.
No facades.
No disillusions.
Being true for the sake of connection.

How do you get there? How do you get to this place of intimacy?

Vulnerability.

We must be vulnerable, no matter how uncomfortable it
may be.
Share your imperfections.
Your fears.
Your doubts.
Your celebrations...with the world.

Hiding the truth from your Self does no good.
No good at all.
Why can't we go home to ourselves?
Are we afraid of what we'll see?
If you don't like what you see, change it and you'll be free.
You can be whoever you want to be as long as you're true.

Who are you?
Who do you want to be?
All you have to do is decide.
Decide who you want to be.
And just be...

Be the person who's open and honest
Be the person who cares to make a difference
Be the person that gives back

And goes back to your Self
Because without going back to your Self
You will not be able to be the person you want to be.

Instead, disconnection is all you'll see.
Disconnection from your Self.
How can you have intimacy if *in* to your Self you can't see?

"*Remembering that shame is the fear of disconnection- the fear that we're unlovable and don't belong- makes it so easy to see why so many people in midlife over-focus on their children's lives, work sixty hours a week, or turn to affairs, addiction, and disengagement. We start to unravel. The messages that fuel shame keep us from fully realizing who we are as people.*"

-Brene Brown, Daring Greatly

Heart Questions

What messages continue to fuel feelings of shame and motivate you to do for others and disconnect with your Self?

What are three ways you can start to come home to yourself and be vulnerable everyday?

What three things can you do to get in touch with your thoughts this week? i.e., meditate, go for a walk, journal.

What three things can you do to get in touch with your feelings this week?

What three things can you do to get in touch with your wants and desires this week?

What do you really want?

What are your dreams?

How can you get your wants and needs met?

What is the first step in getting your wants and needs met?

What can you do this week to get your wants and needs met?

Create a (daily) routine where you incorporate three things you can do to get in touch with your Self i.e., three days a week, on Mondays, Wednesdays, and Fridays I will meditate and journal for thirty minutes to get in touch with myself.

My routine to get in touch with myself will be:

My Promise to Honor My Wants and Needs

Make a promise to yourself to be true to you and what you want and need.

I, _____, promise to be true to myself and honor my thoughts, feelings, wants and needs without judgment. I'm not bad or selfish for having wants and needs. I love myself unconditionally.

Power Statements

I will share my heart and be deeply seen, even when there are no guarantees.
I will come home to myself and love everything I see.

 **Conversation Starters**

How do you love yourself?

How can you be vulnerable and create more intimacy with yourself and people in your life?

Because I Live Inside You

"To see life from the perspective of intuition is to have vision. To see life from the perspective of intuition is to see life from the perspective of wholeness. It is to understand that life is basically one and we are all part of life. While the intellect can only see details. Intuition sees the whole. To see life from the perspective of intuition is like looking at life from the summit of the mountain; whereas seeing life only from the perspective of intellect is like looking at life from the foot of the mountain. Through learning to listen to our intuition, we learn to be in contact with the whole." -Swami Dhyan Giten

Because I Live Inside You

Because I live inside you, I must hear you.
I must listen and not ignore you. You are my guidance.
You are my protector. You're always looking out for my
best interest.

I know you would never hurt me or take me down the
wrong path. You only care about my well being. When I
listen to you, life is perfect.

There is no perfection like the simple joy of the heart. The
pure tenderness of love from the heart- the place where
all love grows.

Love is where we blossom and become who we truly are
with no preconceived notions, expectations, or sadness.

Love is the place of bliss.
The place of connection.
Surrender to authenticity.
Your true nature.
Be loving and kind to yourself.

Do not listen to those voices inside your head telling you to put your guard up, protect yourself, and hide for fear of being seen.

So what if you're really seen? What would that mean- to be really seen?

Sometimes we must ask ourselves what really matters; to be seen or not seen? That is the question.

Stop listening to those questions, those fears, those lies that run rampant inside your head.

They are not friendly. They do not care about you.

They want to hold you back, get in the way of what you really want.

You want to be free but you don't see, listening to your mind and ignoring your heart gets you nowhere you want to be.

You can't be seen for who you truly are when you're hiding in the shackles of your mind. Living in fantasy and fear.

Stand Up! Stand up to your mind.
Tell it, "No! I'm not listening to you anymore! You're stealing my joy with all your fear and worry. You're a drag. You're bringing me down."

You think you're powerless. You think it's hopeless. But what you don't know is your mind has played a funny

trick on you. It's laughing inside your head right now. It's
wish is your command.

All the while your inner knowing, your heart is left at the
curb- lonely for your attention.
Lonely for your tenderness.
Lonely for your love.

Why don't you give your heart some love?
Give yourself some joy.
Listen to the soft voice inside your head you've ignored.

Listen when your heart tells you, "Yes!"
Listen when your heart tells you, "No!"

All you have to do is listen.

Listen to your inner voice.

Heart Questions

How do you consistently listen to your inner critic instead of your heart?

What can you do to turn the volume down on the mind chatter and turn the volume up so you can hear your inner voice?

How do you rationalize ignoring your inner voice?

What positive self-talk statements can you use to motivate you to act on the advice of your inner voice?

Inner Voice Rewards

Create a game for yourself where you reward yourself for honoring your inner voice. Every time you take action and act on your inner voice, by listening to your intuition and "gut," reward yourself in some way. The reward doesn't need to be monetary or extravagant. It does however, need be a reward that makes you feel good about yourself!

Here's a list of rewards you can choose from or you can make up your own. Every time you listen to and act on your inner voice, acknowledge and treat yourself to one or more of the following:

- Bubble bath
- Massage
- Manicure or pedicure
- Jewelry
- Movie
- Nature walk
- Cuddling with your kitty
- Hugging someone you love

- Reading a good book
- Getting your hair done
- Eating out at your favorite restaurant
- Thirty minutes or more of "You" time
- Buy that outfit you've been "eyeing," but not wanting to spend money on yourself

Power Affirmations

When I'm still, I know.
I trust my inner knowing.

 **Conversation Starters**

Have you ever ignored your inner voice and regretted it later?

Why do you listen to your mind instead of your heart?

How can you tell the difference between your mind voice and your intuition?

How can you better honor your gut feelings?

Falling In Love With Yourself

"If you want to awaken all of humanity, then awaken all of yourself. If you want to eliminate the suffering in the world, then eliminate all that is dark and negative in yourself. Truly the greatest gift you have to give is that of your own self-transformation."-Lao Tzu

Falling In Love With Yourself

Fall in love.
Cherish you.

Pamper, care for you.

Be tender to you.
Fill yourself up
With you.

Tell yourself
Sweet nothings.
Nurture yourself, like you would nurture a little girl
The inner child within you.
Fall in love with you.
To your own self be true.

After a decade of research, Brene' Brown, leading expert on shame, authenticity, belonging and wholehearted living, developed the following definition of love:

We cultivate love when we allow our most vulnerable and powerful selves to be deeply seen and known, and when we honor the spiritual connection that grows from that offering with trust, respect, kindness, and affection. We can only love others as much as we love ourselves.

In order for us to truly love- authentically and with our whole heart, we must practice and nurture love for ourselves first.

"As I began to love myself, I freed myself of anything that is no good for my health—food, people, things, situations and everything that drew me down and away from myself. At first I called this attitude a healthy egoism. Today I know it is love of oneself." –Charlie Chaplin

Busy-ness

"Your true home is in the here and now." -Thich Nhat Hanh

Busy-ness

Always rushing here and there
Needing to be somewhere.

Never enough time
You always have to run from one place to the next.
Not enough time to really connect.
Constantly anxious and worried about where you need
to be and do next.
You can't really be present.

You're not here nor there.
You're attention is spread everywhere.
And you're really not anywhere.

Scattered and all over the place
You miss the moments that matter most.
Opportunities for true enjoyment and deep connection
are lost in the constant flutter of busy-ness.

No time to enjoy success, you have to move on to your
next accomplishment.

Precious moments of life, family, and friends lost.

Life passes you by, years wasted saturated with guilt and regret.
Your heart is broken.
Your soul unfulfilled.
Your mind is cluttered with chatter.
You didn't even realize you lost most of your life doing things that don't really even matter.

Heart Questions

Are you busy all the time? How does busy-ness affect your health?

How does busy-ness affect your relationships?

How does busy-ness affect your work, business, and career?

Do you rush from one appointment to the next, one task to the next? If so, how does it affect your mood and the quality of your work?

Do you ever stop to breathe and "smell the roses?"

What could you do to really enjoy the moment?

The definition of being fully present is giving all your attention to what is happening in the *present moment-* during your interactions with others and even when you're alone, not regretting the past or worried about the future.

Do you have difficulty being *fully* present and being one hundred percent emotionally available with your family, friends, co-workers, and clients?

How have difficulties with being *fully* present affected your life, relationships, and work?

Are you easily distracted by your mind and all the things you need to do?

Is it hard for you to focus on what you're doing because you're so busy and rushed all the time?

How can you improve your ability to focus and really appreciate the present moment?

Do you often multi-task throughout your day?

Does multi-tasking cause you to feel anxious or calm?

How can you prioritize your tasks in a way that can bring more calm in your life?

Are you often rushing from one appointment to the next? If so, how can you create more space in your schedule?

What can you start doing right away to create more space in your life and schedule?

Do you get worried and anxious throughout the day thinking about everything you need to do?

Do you take time to chew and savor your food or do you eat quickly so you can get to the next task on your To Do List or next appointment?

Do you take time to really celebrate your accomplishments and achievements? Or do you just keep going on to your next goal, the next goal after that, and the next goal after that until you feel guilty for missing out on things that matter the most to you?

How you can make time in your schedule to celebrate and make time for things that matter the most to you?

What can you do to be fully present in the moment?

Do you take time to really enjoy and be present in your relationships or are you easily distracted and only partially listening when people are talking to you?

Do you take time to nurture your relationships with deep listening, understanding, compassion, and love?

How can you be more attentive, understanding, compassionate, and loving, especially with yourself?

Power Affirmations

Savoring the present moment, I free myself from stress, anxiety, and worry about the past and future.

In this moment, I feel blessed with peace and serenity.

 **Conversation Starters**

How often do you rush from one appointment to the next? One task to the next?

Do you ever take a few moments to just breathe and be in the present moment? What can you do to have less busy-ness in your life?

What are some things you can do to create more space in your life and schedule?

Watering Seeds of Love

Do less.
Feel.
Listen.
Understand.
And Love more.

Being

Duckies swimming so free
happily
not a care in the world.

Content as they are
just to be.

Duckies
just swimming so free
graceful
enchanting
so lovely.

This is what we can strive to be
Peaceful and free.

Happiness in the Present Moment

The past has already gone, and the future has not yet
come.
Let us not drown ourselves in regret for what has passed
or in expectations and worry for the future.

Let us release our sadness and anxiety.
Let us come back to ourselves
and establish ourselves in what is present right now.

Let us learn to recognize
the conditions for happiness
that are present within us and around us.

-Thich Nhat Hanh

Speak Your Truth

"Assertiveness is the courage to show the world our likes and dislikes, our thoughts, feelings, and shortcomings. It's about communicating honestly with family, friends, and colleagues. As we become more assertive, we drop the mask and show our true selves. We proclaim, 'This is who I am, this is what I feel, these are my needs." -Vijaya Sawant

Speak Your Truth

Expressing your wants
your needs
embracing your value.

They say the truth will set you free
But you fear being needy.

Anything to avoid confrontation.

You were taught to people please.
Convinced yourself
that's how to get their approval

Do what they say.
Don't cause any waves.

If you want to be liked,
Tell them what they want to hear.
Avoid being honest to subdue their fears.

All the while, holding your tongue.
Becoming smaller and smaller.
Until the day comes
when you don't even matter.

Speak your truth, it will set you free.
When you do, you'll finally see...
You can get what you want, without being needy.

Margaret's Story

Before working with me, Margaret was a "people-pleasing doormat." She would do anything to avoid people's anger and the possibility of confrontation. Margaret never wanted anyone to feel uncomfortable or cause any waves. She wanted to be liked, even at the expense of compromising her integrity. Never even thinking of speaking her truth for fear of rejection, Margaret had a habit of doing for others and making herself her last priority; this always resulted in over-extending herself and feeling overwhelmed. Every time Margaret did something she didn't really want to do, she would beat herself up for compromising herself and failing to speak her truth.

Empathizing with Margaret and her turmoil, I sought to quickly help her break her "people pleasing" tendencies by supporting her with identifying her emotional triggers, avoidant behavior patterns, and providing her with personalized coaching sessions to help her break through her fears associated with speaking her truth. Then I taught her assertive communication skills to help her finally find her voice. In just a few sessions, Margaret was able to break through the "people pleasing" tendencies that never served her. She beautifully stepped into her power. She felt confident, knowing who she was and what she stood for. She no longer was a "people pleaser" and was able to ask for what she wanted, and get it (to her surprise)!

Every time she spoke her truth with assertive communication, she became more empowered and confident. No longer overwhelmed and weighed down by the negativity of beating herself up, she was able to create the life of her dreams. I loved watching Margaret start up a business doing what she really loved--helping and empowering others while honoring and loving herself. Best of all, she began living life on her terms; no longer a martyr, feeling confident for who she was, and loving herself without the need to be a "people pleasing doormat."

Heart Questions

When have you held your tongue and regretted it later?
What could you have said to honor yourself and speak your truth?
What will you say next time a similar situation presents itself?
Journal about what you want by asking yourself everyday, "What do I really want?"
How can you ask for what you want from your friends, family, and co-workers?

Template for Asking for What You Want:

I feel_____ because_____
and I would really appreciate it if you could _____. It would mean so much to me.

Power Affirmations

I speak my truth readily and easily.
Speaking my truth will set me free.

Conversation Starters

Have there been times when you didn't speak your truth and wished you had?

What happened when you didn't speak your truth?

How do you want to speak your truth and how will you start?

Is it hard for you to speak up and ask for what you want? Do you want to assertively speak your truth and get what you want? Visit www.Janna-Chin.com/Assertive-Skills for Free Assertiveness Tools.

Hard on Yourself

"True abundance isn't based on our net worth, it's based on our self worth." -Gabrielle Bernstien

Hard on Yourself

What does this mean?
To beat yourself up leisurely

No one asks you to do it
You just do it freely.

Whenever you compare yourself
to someone else.

Whenever you discount anything
good you do.

Whenever you put yourself down.

With "I should have's,"
"I should have done better"
But you never do.

Because you're the one
that keeps yourself down.

Thinking you're so unworthy
So undeserving.

Nothing you ever do is good enough.

At least that's what you tell yourself
When you have a pity party.

It's all about me.
Let me spend countless hours
Pointing out my flaws
Woe is me.

I need to be productive, but this
Is what I do leisurely.

I beat myself up.
Because bad habits are hard to break.

And I don't know how to let go of
the inner critic.

It's all about me.
The responsibilities
that I don't live up to.

Because I'm just me.

I don't give myself a break.
This habit is so hard to break.

But what to do?

Something has to give.

Maybe I should start to care about
the inner me

that was wounded
since the beginning.

What can I tell her to soothe
Her pain and worry?

"It's going to be ok my sweet.
There's nothing to fear.
I'm here to soothe away your fears.

I won't let the negativity get you down.
You're so beautiful, even more so when
You're kind to yourself.

There's nothing to regret.
Ever... when you did your best."

Linda's Story

Linda was "stuck." She was so much in a rut that she was sleeping most of her life away and not doing anything all day. Linda came to me because she said she wanted to be a great leader and make a huge difference in the world. However, her business was constipated because of her lack of clarity and brain fog in her head--an unfortunate side effect of chronically beating herself up. I could deeply feel and understand Linda's pain and took her situation to heart. She would tell me in the most exasperated voice, "I want to understand why I'm so stuck and learn the tools to fix it. I want to be more organized and productive so I can grow my business. I want to get out of my head and stop beating myself up all the time!"

After taking Linda through an empowering process to help her break-free of being so hard on herself, Linda was able to "get out of her head" and stop the negativity that had been controlling her life. Once she was able to get the negativity out of her head and let go of the fear, anxiety, worry, and scarcity thinking, she had the clarity she needed to move forward and her confidence skyrocketed to the point where she stepped into her greatest possibility. Using the productivity and organizational tools we co-created for her, she was able to get organized and productive and super-strategic about her business to move her company forward. In the past few years, I've watched Linda become a leader in her industry. What a remarkable thing it is to witness Linda living up to her passion with ease and joy, making a huge contribution to the world.

Heart Questions

How are you hard on yourself?

What are some unkind things you tell yourself when you're upset with yourself?

How do you punish yourself when you don't live up to your own unrealistic expectations?

What are three kind words or positive affirmations you can repeat when you're upset with yourself?

1.
2.
3.

What are three ways you can nurture and love yourself when you make mistakes or don't feel you've lived up to your expectations of perfection?

1.
2.
3.

How can you be kinder to yourself?

What are your positive qualities and strengths? Make a list of at least ten of your positive qualities.

Create five (or more) power affirmations for yourself using your positive qualities and strengths.

1.
2.
3.
4.
5.

Write a letter to your inner five year old. What do you want to say to her? What do you want her to know?

Letter To Your Inner Five Year Old:

Power Affirmations

I'm good enough.
As long as I do my best, my best is good enough.

Conversation Starters

How are you hard on yourself?

What are some unkind things you tell yourself when you're upset with yourself?

What positive self-talk statements can you use to be kinder to yourself?

Mind Chatter

"If you can change your mind. You can change your life." -William James

Mind Chatter

All the conflicting voices in your head.
Old tapes that play over and over.
Until your head starts to spin with dread.
You start to doubt yourself and now
You're filled with worry…overwhelming fear.

Anxiety creeps in
Your heart beats fast
Ba boom
Ba boom.

The chatter is talking to you
telling you
You're not good enough.

There's no point.
Convincing you to give up
Or not even try.
So much time wasted…
All day spinning
Round and round
Over and over.

Beating yourself up.
"I should have done this."
"I should have done that."
"Why didn't I do that?"
"I have to be more prepared."
"I don't know enough."
"I have to try harder."
"I have to be better."

You're not getting much done.
When the chatter keeps coming in.
The volume is so loud
"What if this?" and "What if that?"
Replaying scenarios in your head.

All the chatter reminding you
of all you have to do
Not giving you any rest
It's really taking away from you doing your best.

So much time wasted thinking, thinking
All day and night
Even when you sleep
It's there
Never letting you rest.

You wake up tired.
Exhausted.
Another day
Of being overwhelmed.
Not getting much done
The chatter going
Round and round.

Hounding you
robbing you of joy
Never ending days.
You keep going
Your head keeps spinning
Round and round
Like a merry go round.

You're getting so dizzy
from the sound
Of this never ending chatter
of this crazy
merry go round.

The Sleep Whisperer

I never thought I would become, "The Sleep Whisperer" (as featured in Inside Publications). I always had trouble sleeping ever since I was a little girl. Sleep was not my friend.

I lay awake so many sleepless nights, tossing and turning, thinking, "I need some sleep!"

I lived in my head. Somehow, the fantasies and replays of the day's events were much better when I rewrote the ending or came up with a better story.

"Stop! No, I don't want to listen anymore." But a few minutes would pass and again the obsessing... "What if this?" and "What if that?" coming up with a hundred thousand scenarios of how things could go wrong.

It doesn't help that I let the train wreck go. Toot! Toot! Here comes the train wreck in my head.

Powerless I think I am, but a part of me likes to live in the fantasy, the replays because somehow, I'm in the illusion that I'm in control.

But I'm not.

More sleepless nights.

Fast-forward twenty years.

I wake up and go to the bathroom. I go back to bed, not a care in the world.

Ahhhhh... I love this peaceful place.

How I Found Peace

You may be wondering how I found this peaceful place.

I've learned to turn off the mind chatter and come home to myself.

Florita's Story

Ever since she could remember, Florita was a worry wart. Early on in our work together, she was overweight, barely sleeping, and had noticeable "bags" underneath her eyes. She was also only making a fraction of what she was worth. Being in the health and beauty industry, her health and physical appearance meant everything to her success. Florita was losing business because she was not the model of beauty and health she needed to be to attract clients, and her bank account paid the price. Seeing her in distress, I really felt for Florita and listened intently as she shared her frustrations and I validated her concerns. This client was stressed out and anxious about her money, health, and business. She explained that she learned to worry about money from her mother, and felt hopeless about the possibility of ever being free from the worry, stress, and anxiety that consumed her nearly all the time. All of these emotions and thoughts comprised the mind chatter that negatively affected every aspect of her life.

Empathizing with Florita's turmoil and desire to change, I took her through a process of understanding her emotional triggers for worry and anxiety. Then we co-created tools to assist her with coping with stress in the moment of her stress triggers, and developed power affirmations she could use to shift her mindset. After just one powerful session, I could tell Florita was sleeping well and the bags underneath her eyes were disappearing. She was much more energetic and alive. She was filled with excitement when she shared with me that she had experienced a significant reduction in stress, worry, and anxiety. Florita was noticing her emotional triggers, using her coping skills and shifting her mindset and felt much lighter. She could see the "light at the end of the tunnel."

Florita stopped her obsessive behaviors and was able to relax, have fun, and was happy for the first time in a long time. She was also spending quality time with her boyfriend and felt inspired, motivated, and ready to go out into the world to grow her business. Instead of hiding out at home as she had been doing for months, Florita achieved her professional goal with renewed vitality and inspiration. I was happy to see Florita live her dream. She earned a bonus all-expense paid trip to Hawaii within a few months of completing our work together!

Florita's story illustrates so well that when you're able to let go of all the worry and anxiety caused by incessant mind chatter, you too, will experience peace, inspiration, and restful nights.

In the next section, I share with you the process I created that has given me and many of my clients peace of mind. It is the same exercise I take my clients through to help them find peace from incessant mind chatter that keeps them up at night and worried during the day; this process powerfully takes women from feeling overwhelmed to feeling hopeful, calm and focused.

Heart Questions

1. Think about a worry or fear that keeps coming up for you. It could be anything like, "How am I going to get through my To Do List?" or "How am I going to be able to pay the bills?" which are common worries. Write down your fear(s) or worry.

Fear/Worry One:

Fear/Worry Two:

2. Write down the opposite of your fear or worry. The opposite of your fear or worry- meaning what it would look like when your fear or worry is resolved.

3. List three times or situations when your fear or worry never came true.

a)
b)
c)

Create a positive affirmation, or positive self-talk for the opposite of your worry- a statement that you can say to yourself that makes you feel calm for each of your worries.

Example positive affirmations:

"Things always work out for me."

"My To Do List always gets done."

4. Repeat the positive affirmations and self-talk over and over until you start believing it.

Here's what it looks like when this exercise is completed:

a) Fear: "How am I going to get everything done on my To Do List?"

b) Opposite of your fear: "Everything will get done on my To Do List"

d) Example of a time when your fear didn't come true:

"I completed the most important things that needed to get done today and it all worked out."

d) Positive affirmation to repeat to yourself when you're afraid and overwhelmed by your To Do List.

For example, "Things always work out for me even when the To Do List is incomplete."

Power Affirmations

I'm a beautiful, lovable, and worthwhile person.
I am enough.
I'm good enough even when I make mistakes.
Everything I've asked for the Universe has already lined up for me.

Conversation Starters

How does mind chatter affect your work, productivity, and well-being?

What can you do to calm the chatter in your head and experience peace, and joy?

Do you want to get control of your mind chatter? Do you want peace of mind? Visit www.Janna-Chin.com/Mind-Chatter for more Free tools.

Losing Your Identity

Losing Your Identity

Have you ever lost yourself in love?
Given up everything
For love.

Prioritized his wants
Before your own.

Forgotten to even have wants.
When he asks you, "What do you want?"
You honestly don't know.

For so long, you've been lost
In a sea of all about him
That you don't even realize what you've done.

You've become a doormat
An empty shallow excuse for
a reason to exist.

You tell yourself, it's all about him
I have nothing without him.

Yes, this has become true
Maybe that's why you're so blue.

Boundaries

"Boundaries are a part of self-care. They are healthy, normal, and necessary." -Doreen Virtue

Boundaries

They don't teach you in school
Parents may not know what to do to show you.

Where do you learn to set limits on your time
Your emotions
Your body and soul?

When someone is monologuing
And you have to go...

What do you say?
You don't want to be rude.

When someone plays with your emotions
How do you care for your heart?

Do you give away your body and your soul
And settle for the physical
Instead of being kind to your heart?

You could tell them from the start
your expectations
So they don't break your heart.

Angie's Story

Before working with me, Angie was not only overwhelmed and exhausted, but she was also physically ill. She was receiving treatment for stress-related symptoms from her doctor several times a week, and was a "frequent flyer" at the hospital. Angie had been a stay-at-home mom for over fifteen years, and for the first time in her life, she had to balance motherhood with being a business woman and entrepreneur. Her husband had been the primary financial provider and his income was in jeopardy. Angie was feeling tremendous pressure to "bring home the bacon." She was wracked with guilt for what she believed to be neglecting her children because she was so busy working and helping everyone else, that she had little time for herself--let alone quality time with her kids.

Angie came to me because she wanted to get out of overwhelm, have a healthy work life balance, improve her health, and grow her business so she could financially contribute to her family. After learning more about Angie and taking her through an enlightening process of understanding her "Overwhelm Cycle," we learned that Angie was overwhelmed because she had too much on her plate due to her inability to say "No" to anyone in need. Her heart was bigger than her 'Superwoman' abilities. From the time she woke up in the morning, until the time she passed out from exhaustion in the evening, every minute of every day was filled with things she had to do--most of which were self-imposed commitments she felt obligated to follow through on as a result of not setting boundaries for self-care. Angie admitted with dismay that she didn't know how to set boundaries to take care of herself, or manage her time which was the cause of her feeling chronically overwhelmed, guilt-ridden, and exhausted. She also felt a deep sense of shame for not knowing how to juggle all of this.

First we discovered Angie's emotional triggers. Then we co-created personalized scripts to set boundaries using assertive communication. In addition, I provided her with breakthrough coaching sessions to free her from guilt. Angie was able to break her overwhelm cycle by setting boundaries and taking care of herself. By prioritizing herself first, she improved her health to the point where she had nearly no physical symptoms of stress. Angie was spending quality time with her family, and enjoying a healthy work life balance, while growing her income and business.

During the past year, I have seen Angie blossom and really come into her own. I am so proud of Angie for all that she has accomplished and am honored to have been a part of her life. Today, Angie's business and income has grown exponentially. Not only is she an amazing, heart-centered leader who supports a team of over two hundred women, she contributes financially to her family and gives back to the community--not as guilt-ridden 'Superwoman,' but as the best version of herself.

Heart Questions

Have you ever felt like a "doormat," like someone walked all over you and took advantage of your kindness?

Did you clearly communicate to them with your words and actions how you wanted to be treated?

What can you say and do next time to clearly communicate with your words and actions how you'd like to be treated?

Have you ever done anything or went out of your way to please someone (even when you didn't want to) because you wanted to be liked and accepted? If yes, write down and process some of your experiences.

How did you feel about yourself?

How did people pleasing affect your self-esteem and confidence?

How did people pleasing affect your life and livelihood?

How did people pleasing affect your relationships?

How did people pleasing affect your business?

Have you ever had sex with someone when you wanted love, but settled for sex instead?

How do you want to feel about yourself?

What are three things you can do to start setting some limits on how you want to be treated?

What are three things you can do to start setting some limits on how you want to treat yourself?

Power Affirmations

Today, I will honor myself and speak my truth.
I will let go of fear and ask for what I want.
I'm not willing to settle for less. I deserve the best.

 ## Conversation Starters

What are boundaries and what do they mean to you?

When you were growing up, were you taught boundaries?

What did your parents and authority figures teach you about trusting, speaking up, and taking care of yourself?

How can you set limits to take care of yourself physically, emotionally, and spiritually?

Are setting healthy boundaries difficult for you? Do you want to learn how to set loving boundaries? Visit www.Janna-Chin.com/boundaries for free more free tools.

Pride

"Pride is spiritual cancer. It eats up the very possibility of love, or contentment, or even common sense." -C. Lewis

Pride

Pride wants to be free.
It wants you to see
what it wants you to see.
Sometimes in illusion
We're in the dark wanting, wanting to look like we got it
going on.
We know what we're doing.

We keep going on wanting to be right.
It's so very important.
It must be done our way
pride's voice says.

No apologies here.
Admitting I was wrong, this I just can't bare.

Pride.

It can be light or dark.
The choice is yours.

Heart Questions

Have you ever stayed in an unhealthy relationship with a partner or employer because of pride? Write down and process your feelings about what happened.

Have you ever felt the need to be right even when it was causing conflict in your relationship? How did ego pride get in the way of having a harmonious relationship?

Have you ever had a hard time saying sorry because of ego pride?

How has ego pride caused rifts in your relationships?

Was it worth it to be right?

Was it worth it not to apologize?

How did not apologizing affect your relationships?

In retrospect, what would you do differently if you could have done things differently?

What will you do differently in the future?

What would it mean about you if you admitted you were wrong?

What would the benefits be for saying sorry? List them.

Could apologizing bring you closer to the people you care about?

If ego wasn't pressuring you to do it your way or be right, how would you want your work and relationships to be like?

How has ego pride affected your work? Describe how ego pride encourages you to work endless hours striving for perfection?

How does ego pride affect your self-esteem when you continue to work on projects for the sake of growing your ego? What expense do you pay to grow and feed your ego pride?

What would your life be like if you had healthy pride and stood up for yourself when you're mistreated?
What is your definition of healthy pride?
What would healthy pride look like in your work and relationships?
What three things can you do to start cultivating healthy pride in your work and relationships?

Power Affirmations

I love myself enough to let go of ego pride. Ego pride no longer serves me.
My strong work ethic is my new healthy pride.

 **Conversation Starters**

What do you think is the difference between healthy and unhealthy pride (ego pride)?

What will you do the next time ego pride comes between you and your relationships? How can you create a win/win situation?

She Wants

"Once when I was running, from all that haunted me;
to the dark I was succumbing- to what hurt unbearably.
Searching for the one thing, that would set my sad soul
free. In time, I stumbled upon it, an inner calm and peace;
and now I am beginning, to see and to believe, in who
I am becoming- and who I've yet to be." -Lang Leav

She Wants

She wants love so desperately.
But she's unsure.

Unsure if she can get it.
Fearful of the unknown.

She doesn't know
what he's thinking
What he's wanting.

She wants to know
If it's possible
To trust this man
Who's so unknown.

He looks at her inquisitively
To see
What's in her eyes that
Seeks him so desperately.

She seems so lonely
There must be a reason
for her loneliness.

He wonders
Can he be her answer.

There's so much yearning
In her eyes
She really tries.

Desperately she's trying
To get his attention
With siren red lipstick.

She wants his attention
And affection.

The look in her eyes is
almost haunting.
Begging for his love.

Just caught up in fantasy.
She wants. She wants.

Heart Questions

Have you ever wanted something or someone so much you were willing to compromise yourself to get what you wanted?

Have you ever agreed to sex when you really wanted love? How did it make you feel about yourself?

How do you want to feel in a relationship?

How do you want to be treated in a relationship?

What have you been settling for?

How have you settled for less?

How do you justify settling for less?

What is your relationship pattern? Do you have the tendency to have the same kinds of relationships over and over?

What are you willing to accept?

How can you value yourself so others value you?

How can you fall in love with yourself and love yourself more than you've ever loved anyone before?

What's getting in the way of you loving yourself first?

What are the old tapes that keep playing in your head that keeps you from loving yourself first?

If you could re-write your love story, what would your love story look and feel like?

Re-write your love story in your journal-- allow the words to simply flow without analyzing or judging your thoughts or feelings.

Power Affirmations

I'm good enough.
I love myself unconditionally.

I love me first. It's not selfish or greedy. It's necessary.

 **Conversation Starters**

How can you value yourself?

What needs to happen for you to fall in love with yourself first, more than anyone you've loved before?

Is it possible to love yourself first and not be selfish, but more loving?

How can you be more loving to yourself?

Judgment

"Love is the absence of judgment." -Dalai Lama

Judgment

Judging yourself and others
Does this ever lead to possibilities?
Harsh and unkind, your judgements can be
Leaving you defeated and fearful of the unforeseen.

Most of the time the voice of judgment is critical
Nit-picky and rips away hope for possibilities.

It's the voice of disparagement, hopelessness, and non-acceptance of who your heart and soul want you to be.

Does your heart yearn for intimate connection and peace?
Let your heart be the guide that leads you to peace and serenity.

Heart Questions

How do you judge yourself?

What are some unkind judgments that comes to mind when you judge yourself and others?

How do these judgements make you feel?

How do you want to feel?

What could you say to judgment to set yourself free from its harsh criticisms?

How do you want to see yourself and others?

What three things can you do to start being less judgmental of yourself?

What three things can you do to start being less judgmental of others?

What can you do to keep yourself accountable for these three steps for letting go of judgment of yourself and others?

Power Affirmations

It's not good or bad. It just is (what it is).

Letting go of judgment, I accept myself and others as they are.

Loving myself and others, I let go of the tendency to judge and set myself free from harsh criticism that no longer serves me.

 **Conversation Starters**

Do you have the tendency to be hard on yourself? If so, how are you hard on yourself?

Do you find yourself comparing yourself to others and feeling like you don't measure up?

How is comparing and judging yourself helpful to you?

How can you start to let go of judgment of yourself and others and love yourself more?

Anger and Resentment

An old Cherokee told his grandson, "My son, there is
a battle between two wolves inside us all. One is evil.
It is anger, jealousy, greed, resentment, inferiority, lies,
and ego. The other is good. It is joy, peace, love, hope,
humility, kindness, empathy, and truth. The boy thought
about it and asked, "Grandfather, which wolf wins?"

The old man quietly replied, "The one you feed."

Anger and Resentment

It will eat away at you
The anger simmers within
Your blood boils and
Suddenly
Kaboom!

Like a hurricane,
out of nowhere
You need someone to blame.

You're stewing in bitterness
"How dare they?"

Don't they know all that I do?
Appreciation is all I ask and I can't even get that.

I'll make them pay.

Doors slam
Voices raise
Pots fly
And then...

Your demands.

Now they must pay.
You want them to know all that you've done.
All your sacrifice.

You hold them hostage with your anger and resentment,
Accusations and judgments.
When you know what?

They never asked anything of you in the first place.

You did it all on your own and now you want someone
to blame.

You didn't get what you wanted.

You didn't do it for them out of the kindness of your heart.

You had unspoken conditions and expectations.

Now your anger and resentment eats away at you.
No longer is there peace in your heart.
If only you were honest with your intentions from the
start.

*"Hanging on to resentment is like letting someone you despise
live rent free in your head."* –Ann Landers

Even though the idea of being a martyr has negative connotations most of us would prefer not to associate ourselves with, if you often experience feelings of anger and resentment, you may want to take to heart the definition of a martyr.

Martyrs are victimized not so much by others as they victimize themselves. When you feel anger and resentment, you may not realize that you actually participated in your own victimization by doing any or all of the following:

1. Doing something you really didn't want to do
2. Meeting people's needs without being asked
3. Sacrificing your wants and needs to please others
4. Doing something for someone when they should be doing it for themselves

The first step in breaking free from the negative feelings and consequences of anger, resentment, and overwhelm is to acknowledge you have the tendency to sacrifice your emotional, physical, and/or spiritual well-being for the sake of others before loving and taking care of yourself. The following heart questions will guide you to work through your tendency to put others first.

Heart Questions

How have you participated in your own victimization?

What were you hoping to gain from doing something for others when they should be doing it themselves?

1.
2.
3.

Why do you do for others when they should be doing it themselves?
Are you really helping them if you do it for them when they can do it themselves?
What do you think you want and need from them?

How can you meet your needs for _____,
instead of doing for others when they should be doing it themselves?

What three things can you do to meet your needs for _____?

Three things I can do to meet my own needs:

1.
2.
3.

What were you hoping to gain from meeting people's needs without being asked?

How have you sacrificed your wants and needs to please others?

How have you perpetuated anger and resentment by meeting people's needs without being asked?

Why did you do something you didn't want to do?

What can you do instead of compromising your integrity and comfort to please others?

How can you please and make yourself happy?

How can you ask for what you want instead of pleasing others?

What will you do next time someone asks you to do something you don't want to do?

Power Affirmations

Letting go of anger and resentment, I feel a huge weight lifted from me.

Anger and resentment no longer serves me. I now vibrate at a higher frequency. I'm liberated and totally free.

 **Conversation Starters**

Have you ever met someone's needs without being asked and then became angry and resentful when they didn't appreciate you?

What can you do to take care of you instead of focusing on others?

No Appreciation

No Appreciation

No appreciation when you feel cheated and disregarded.

There's no gratitude for what you've done- all that you've
done for them.
They take you for granted because they don't realize
the true value of what you've given them.

It's whatever to them.
Leaving you feeling bitter and resentful.

You took care of them, the least they could do is appreciate
you for all you do.
You've done so much.
Given so much.

Why can't they realize what you've done for them?
Why does it matter so much?
Why is it so important to you anyway?

These are questions worth asking yourself.

Doing for others brings little reward when you're seeking
to receive in return.

Appreciation is payment for services rendered without their agreement in the first place.

Free yourself from the appreciation trap.
It's ok if they don't give a crap.

Shame

"The difference between shame and guilt is the difference between 'I am bad' and 'I did something bad." -Brene Brown

Shame

It's like a nasty pain
that's hard to tame.

Once it's got a hold of you
It digs deep into your soul.

It's cold and unforgiving
It adds ten thousand pounds of salt
to your deepest wounds.

And it's so hard to set yourself free.

You feel so stupid.
How could you be so selfish and inconsiderate.

You're convinced you're terrible.
Oh the taste of shame is harsh, beyond bitter,
relentless, unbearable
and leaves the most disgusting after taste.

It tells you you're bad
fills you with regret and keeps you trapped in self-defeat.
Now you don't believe in you.

Your confidence is blown.
Your head is down and you're really low.

Shame has got you tamed.
What can you do?

Beat shame at it's own game.
Unleash your warrior woman
Bust out a can of Whoop Ass
and put shame in it's place.

Be a Freakin Bad Ass
Why?
Because kicking ass beats lame ass shame.

Heart Questions

What situations or experiences causes or triggers you to feel guilty and ashamed?

What is the energy of shame in your life? Describe the affects of guilt and shame in your life.

What negative self-talk do you repeatedly hear yourself saying to yourself over and over when something happens to trigger your feelings of guilt and shame?

How have you bought into other people's projections and taken on their guilt and shame?

What happens to your body when you feel ashamed? Do you feel heavy or light? Do you get hot and start to sweat? Does your heart start to beat really fast? How does your body respond to feelings of shame?

What can you do to let go of shame?

What positive self-talk could you say to yourself in the moment to let go of guilt and shame and instead, cherish and create loving thoughts and feelings for yourself when shame rears it's ugly head?

What tangible actions can you commit to doing everyday to love yourself more?

Power Affirmations

I'm tired of shame's lame ass game and I will no longer let it control me.

Letting go of guilt and shame, I set myself Free!

Conversation Starters

Do you ever feel ashamed?

Sharing your vulnerabilities helps you to love and accept yourself more. What burdens have you been carrying with you?

What does shame tell you about yourself?

How does shame turn into guilt and turmoil and what would you rather experience instead?

What will you do to let go of guilt and shame?

Disappointment

"Expectation is the root of all heartache." –William Shakespeare

Disappointment

It's a feeling of sadness
Deep down in the pit of your stomach
Like someone punched you in the gut

And dissed you at the same time.

It feels like the message was,
"I don't give a shit about you"
I didn't even care enough to follow through
Or give a damn to say "yes" to you.

It hits the core of your essence
Brings up your insecurities
All your self-doubts and fears.

You may even question, "Am I lovable?
Is there something wrong with me?
Why did they reject me?"

What would seem like a simple disappointment
to others
Is a catastrophe for you.
Almost the end of the world
at the very least, leaves you with the feeling

of bitter dissatisfaction
A longing that was totally unsatisfied
Which leaves you wondering...

Why were your expectations so high
When time and time again, people disappoint.
You tell yourself, "You should have known better."

The best way to let go of disappointment
Even though it's not what you want to hear,
is simple yet difficult to do.

Let go.

Let go of expectation.

Let go of attachment to outcomes.

And everything you receive will be a happy surprise.
A gift you didn't even expect
A reward for just doing your best.

Heart Questions

Have you ever been disappointed?

What does it feel like when you're disappointed?

Have you been disappointed often in your life?

Did your parents and significant people in your life keep their promises to you?

How have you shied away from taking risks and fully living for fear of being disappointed?

How can you better cope with disappointment so it no longer debilitates your growth or negatively impacts your self-esteem and confidence?

What can you do to self-soothe yourself when you experience disappointment?

How can you be objective about the situation (separate past experiences and disappointments from the current situation)?

What can you do to stop taking it personally when people don't follow through or break promises?

What can you do to let go of expectations and experience more peace and serenity?

How can you love and accept people more than you already do?

What are three possible reasons why someone may have failed to follow through on their promise to you?

What could have been happening in their lives to cause them to break their promise to you?

What could they have been going through at the time?

When you feel disappointed, cultivating understanding and compassion for others will help you find peace and deepen your self-love and love for others.

Power Affirmations

In the midst of disappointment, I will rise high.
Learning from my mistakes, I grow deeper in my commitment for self-love and compassion for others.
I become more than I think I can be, by looking beyond what I presently believe.

 **Conversation Starters**

How does disappointment affect you?

How have you allowed disappointment to affect your ability to take risks and live a deeper, more fulfilling life?

How can you self-soothe and reassure your inner child?

Letting Go

"Letting go doesn't mean you stop caring. It means you stop trying to force others to." –Mandy Hale

Letting Go

Letting go of control I know my heart will find peace.

I release expectations and the need to be right and do it my way.

No more disappointments.

No more heartache.

Heart Questions

Do you feel being in control has been an issue for you?
How have you tried to control people, situations, and outcomes?
How has trying to prove you're right stolen your peace of mind?
How has trying to control and convince people to do it your way stolen your peace mind?
How has trying to control people, situations, and outcomes caused you stress, anxiety and worry?
How has trying to control people, situations, and outcomes affected your health and happiness?
What are three things you can you do to start "letting go" and experiencing happier, healthier relationships with yourself and others?

Power Affirmations

Today I let go of the need to control and set myself free from stress, anxiety, and worry.
Choosing peace and serenity, I let go and let God carry out his perfect plan for me.

Conversation Starters

What are you holding onto that is no longer serving you?

What's the first step you're going to take to start letting go of what's no longer serving you?

Peace

"Peace. It does not mean to be in a place where there is no trouble, noise, or hard work. It means to be in the midst of those things and still be calm in your heart." -Lady Ga Ga

Peace

The place of calm and serenity.
The place where we feel whole
With no fears
No worries
No doubts.

Peace is a place of self-acceptance and love.

Peace is a place where we trust ourselves
And take care of things that really matter...
To us.

Peace is being true to ourselves
No matter what the consequences.

It's having the inner knowing of
Following our
integrity
Quietly
Silently
being true to ourselves
When no one notices

But you know, and feel that
Inner calm and peace
Inside your heart
Feeling so peaceful and
Tender in your own heart.

Loving yourself unconditionally
Where the opinions of others don't
Really matter
Because you're truly free
With an inner peace
And tranquility
That brings a smile to your face
You have been in the muck of the mud
And now, you are the beautiful lotus
Floating
On the water
So serene.

Heart Questions

Have you ever felt at peace? How can you duplicate the peaceful feeling you (once) felt?

How can you get to a place of peace in your heart?

What expectations of yourself or others are you hoping to come true that steal your sence of peace?

How do you manage disppointments?

Do you feel devasted by the disapointments you experience?

How can you manage your disappointments so that the disappointments you experience don't cause you deep hurt and emotional pain?

How does caring about other people's opinions of you take away from your sense of peace?

How can you start to value your own opinion over other people's opinion of you?

How do you think valuing your own opinion over others will help you find peace?

What can you do to create space in your home or office to allow more peace into your environment?

Are there relationships in your life that cause you to experience stress?

How can you detach from these stressful relationships for your own health and wellness?

What are three things you can start doing to bring more peace into your life?

Power Affirmations

I am peace.
Peace is in my heart.

Connecting with my breath, I can find peace at any moment.

 **Conversation Starters**

When are you not at peace?

What does peace mean to you?

How can you find peace?

Money Business and Financial Abundance

Fear and
Self-Sabotage

"When I dare to be powerful, to use my strength in the service of my vision, then it becomes less and less important whether I am afraid." -Audre Lorde

Fear and Self-Sabotage

Is when you know you should do something
But you don't.

You find excuses
Procrastinate
Distract yourself.

Waste time
Spin yourself in circles
Avoid
Delay
Question.

Ask everyone else what they think
Don't trust yourself.
Don't believe in yourself.
Do enough just to get by.

Self-sabotage.
Fail to meet deadlines.
Don't do your best.

Fail your own test.

Time after time
It's the same deal
You spin yourself around the wheel.

Then wonder why...
Maybe because you let success pass you by
While you were too busy listening to fear's lies.

"Our deepest fear is not that we are inadequate. Our deepest fear is that we are powerful beyond measure. It is our light, not our darkness that most frightens us. We ask ourselves, 'Who am I to be brilliant, gorgeous, talented, fabulous?' Actually, who are you not to be? You are a child of God. Your playing small does not serve the world. There is nothing enlightened about shrinking so that other people won't feel insecure around you. We are all meant to shine, as children do. We were born to make manifest the glory of God that is within us. It's not just in some of us; it's in everyone. And as we let our own light shine, we unconsciously give other people permission to do the same. As we are liberated from our own fear, our presence automatically liberates others."

-Marianne Williamson, A Return to Love: Reflections on the Principles of "A Course in Miracles"

Heart Questions

What are you afraid of?
How has fear prevented your success in life and business?
What is the one thing you've been wanting to do, but have not done yet?
How will facing your fears bring you closer to your goal(s)?
What is one small action you can take to face your fears?
What is one action step you can take to bring you closer to your goals?

Fearless Exercise

List all your fears on a piece separate piece of paper.

Once you've listed all your fears, participate in this ritual to liberate yourself from fear.

1. Take a pen and cross out all your fears
2. Crumple up the paper with all your fears
3. Repeat out loud the Power Statements below (or create your own Power Statements)
4. Throw away your crumpled up fears in the garbage and commit to letting them go forever.

Power Statements

When I feel fear, I'm going to feel the fear and do it anyway. Fear no longer serves me, knowing this; I choose to set myself free.

Fear no longer has a hold of me. I'm liberating myself from fear and in doing so, my presence will liberate others. My light will shine so bright.

 **Conversation Starters**

What fears have been keeping you from "playing" big in the world?

How does fear keep you from shining your light?

What are three action steps you can do to start taking more risks?

Fear of Success and Failure

"You gain strength, courage and confidence by every experience in which you really stop to look fear in the face… you must do the one thing you think you cannot do." -Eleanor Roosevelt

Fear of Success and Failure

You have no idea
About this fear

How it controls you
Holds you back
From taking charge
Really going for it...

You tell yourself
I'm not prepared
I don't know enough
All the responsibility
I'd rather
leave that to others; the best

I have to keep doing
What I'm doing.
Asking everybody else
Wasting time
Distracting myself
Guilt tripping myself.

One foot forward
Two steps back on the brakes

Stop go.
Stop go.

You're so close
to getting to your next level.

You can taste it.
You can feel it.
In your body.
In your bones.

But then, self-sabotage.
You stop yourself from
Really going for it.
More excuses.
More distractions.

A never ending cycle of
Guilt, shame, and despair

What are you going to do
To break through this fear?

Get a hold of yourself.

Stop playing it safe.
Just go for it.

If you don't, you don't
have anyone to blame

And will feel the shame.

There will be regret
Your life and business
will be put to the test.

Don't give up!
You're better than all the rest.

All you have to do is your best.
And you will beat
Fear of success.

Heart Questions

Would you rather not take risks so you stay comfortable where you're at? Why?

Are you afraid of not knowing enough?

Are you afraid of the unexpected?

Do you have a fear of being amazingly successful? If yes, what do you fear?

How would your life change if you were amazingly successful?

Do you deserve to be successful or is amazing success only reserved for special people?

How has fear of success been holding you back from achieving more success?

Are you afraid of taking on more responsibility if you get to your next level? If yes, why?

Do you fear you're not going to be able to cope with more success? If yes, why?

How will you handle amazing success? What do you need to have in place to be prepared for amazing success?

Do you second guess yourself often? If yes, why? What can you do about it?

Do you distract yourself often to avoid doing what you know will get you to your next level? Identify some examples.

What do you have in common with someone you respect who has already achieved a goal similar to yours?

What obstacles are in your way and how can you start to overcome them?

What do you need to change to achieve your goals?

Releasing Resistance

If you haven't made the changes you know would benefit your life, there's a reason: you're consciously or unconsciously resisting making this change. Even though you may not be aware of your resistance, it's important to free-write about why you aren't making these important changes. It could as simple as, "I don't know" or it could be more complicated. You might be thinking, "If I change and play big, I might outgrow my friends and family and they might not love me anymore."

Write down any resistance you have about doing what you know is good for your life and business. By doing this exercise, you can discover what the resistance is about and release it.

Why are you resisting making important changes for your health, happiness, and/or financial well-being?

Are these fears about making changes real?
Is fear of change holding you back?
How could you prepare yourself to step into greater possibilities in your life and business?
What are some takeaways you learned by answering these questions?
What action steps are you going to take to break-free from fear of success and failure so you can live your best life?

Power Affirmations

I will do the one thing I think I can not do.

Today, I'm breaking up with fear and forging towards the greatness in me.

 **Conversation Starters**

How do you get in your own way?

What do you plan to do to get out of your own way?

Playing It Safe

"I don't want an uneventful and safe life, I prefer an adventurous one." -Isabel Allende

Playing It Safe

"I'm keeping you safe"
That's what your mind tells you
Convinces you
To stop in your tracks.
Right where you are so
You stay safe.

Stuck in safety.
Never going farther.
Spinning in circles.
Playing it safe.

Taking a chance
Any kind of risk
Is a "No, No."

You won't be safe anymore.
Out of your comfort zone,
You will be in danger of incredible growth
And amazing possibilities.

But your mind has convinced you to stay the same
Play it safe.

It's main purpose... to stunt your growth.
Steer you away from your heart's desires and passions.

There are no riches in the safety of your cocoon.

All the diamonds and jewels await you when
You transform into a beautiful butterfly
And fly high.

Serena's Story

Before working with me, Serena sabotaged her life and business. Over the years, she lost over $100k because she had a fear of success and failure that sabotaged her success; She always played it safe. The idea of taking a risk would nearly give her a panic attack. Because she was consumed with fear nearly all the time, Serena was depressed and often isolated herself. Abandoned by her family at a young age, Serena sought security and safety with the familiar. She fiercely held onto money and relationships-even when the relationships were unhealthy. Serena rarely spent money on services or experiences that could make her life easier. She was trapped in hopelessness and fear. I could feel the pain and depression through Serena's demeanor. I was fully committed to helping her live an empowered life.

During our work together, I helped Serena let go of her fears related to money and educated her on the effects of scarcity and fear-based thinking. I also taught her how to have a healthy money mindset. Serena and I co-created a simple and empowering, strategic rewards plan that provided her with tangible steps she could take and tools she could use to overcome her fears.

With empowered tools and support, she was able to free herself of self-sabotage, move past her fears (and habit of playing it safe), and get her mojo back! She was able to take strategic risks and create a life of deep meaning, contribution, and abundance helping others. Most importantly and this is what thrilled me the most, Serena was finally able to love and trust. She found joy in heartfelt personal and professional relationships that not only enriched her life, but also grew her business and income. She was finally able to enjoy financial freedom and travel the world.

Heart Questions

How have you been playing it safe?

What thoughts and self-talk has your mind made up to keep you safe and away from your highest potential?

List the thoughts and self-talk that have kept you from experiencing more success and/or the life you really want?

What are the opposite of those limiting thoughts and self-talk?

Create a list of at least ten uplifting and expansive thoughts (opposite of your limiting thoughts) and positive self-talk statements that will help you feel courageous and empowered.

Courage Cards

Create "Courage Cards" by writing your empowered self-talk phrases on index cards and post-it notes. Keep your Courage Cards near you and can easily see them: in your purse, near your bed, in the bathroom mirror (and anywhere else in your home, car, and surroundings where you frequent often.) Read each Courage Card daily ten times a day until you start believing your empowered affirmations and they become automatic thoughts.

Power Affirmations

Today I have the courage to face my fears and take one step closer to my goal(s).

I'm no longer going to playing it safe. From now on, I'm choosing to fully live with more ease, joy and adventure!

 **Conversation Starters**

How have you been playing it safe?

What are the disadvantages of playing it safe? What adventures and opportunities have you missed out on because you've been playing it safe?

Do you want an uneventful and safe life or do you want a life filled with passion, love and adventure?

What are you going to do to start taking some risks so you can live the life you really want?

Procrastinating In The Way

"Nothing is so fatiguing as the eternal hanging on of an uncompleted task." -Don Marquis

Procrastinating In The Way

There's always reasons why
You find excuses not to even try
To do what needs to be done.

It's a way you find to run
From the things that are important to do
Yet you always find an excuse.

Time starts to tick
And there's so much to do
Everything's piling up
And yet you still procrastinate.

Wasting time to wait
Until the last minute
Before you know it, it's the due date.

Anxiety comes
From all that needs to be done
To catch up from
The piles of work

That took so much more time to get done.

Guilt starts to peak it's dirty face
Telling you you're a disgrace.

You waited until the last minute
and now it may be too late
All because you procrastinate.

Create Your Stop Procrastinating Action Plan

Step One: Think about what your procrastination habits are. What excuses or reasons do you tell yourself to avoid those projects?

What are the excuses you tell yourself to justify procrastinating?

What are the reasons you use to justify procrastinating?

Step Two: How do you procrastinate?

What are your avoidance behaviors that distract you from completing important tasks or projects?

Make a list of your avoidant behaviors:

Step Three: Write down the main activities you engage in when you procrastinate and identify specific steps you can take to overcome your procrastinating habits.

Activities you engage in when you procrastinate i.e., surfing the internet, checking Facebook and e-mails, doing laundry:

Action steps you can take to stop procrastinating:

Stop Procrastination Action Plan

Set your intention at the beginning of each day to be laser focused. For example, I will be laser focused and complete three prioritized projects by 5pm today.

Instead of _____

I will _____

when I feel the urge to distract myself from important tasks.

Power Affirmations

I'm getting it done today.
I'm just going to do it!

 **Conversation Starters**

How do you procrastinate?

How does procrastination get in the way of your success?

What three action steps can you start doing to stop procrastinating?

Resistance

"Paralyze resistance with persistence." -Woody Hayes

Resistance

A feeling of dread
lacking the desire
To engage
And move forward.

Some may even say
A stubbornness
Of avoiding
And steadfast
Determination
Not to do something.

You may not know what it is
That's holding you back
You may not even be aware
That you're holding
Yourself back

Your unconscious ego
Is safeguarding you from
the possibility of success
It wants to play it safe
So there's no chance
You can make a fool of the all too sensitive ego.

Your ego can't take the criticism so it's trying to protect
You from the possibility of failure.

But you don't even know what's going on...

All you know is that you're resisting
With dread
Doing the things that involve risk
And getting out of your comfort zone
That could really help you get to
where you want to go.
But you're not really sure if you want it
Big success that is...
So you resist
Back and forth you go.
One step forward
Two steps back
In the "I'm safe game"
Of your so called life.

Heart Questions

What have you been resisting?
Why have you been resisting this situation and not taking action?
Would you be experiencing more peace, success, and happiness if you stopped resisting?
How has resistance kept you from experiencing more success?
What is resistance in your body telling you?
What is your heart trying to tell you about this resistance?
What would happen if you stopped resisting?
Is there any fear behind your resistance?
What can you do to push past the fear?
How can you distinguish between healthy resistance and fear-based resistance?
How can you let go of fear-based resistance and experience more peace, joy, and success?

Power Affirmations

When resistance appears, I know my heart is pointing me in the right direction. I will paralyze resistance with persistence.
I'm letting go of resistance and peacefully allowing my life to unfold.

Conversation Starters

Have you experienced fear-based resistance in any area of your life?

How has fear-based resistance kept you from experiencing more success in your life, work, and relationships?

Sales and Fear of Rejection

*"Rejection doesn't mean you're not good enough.
It means the other person failed to notice
what you had to offer." -Mark Amend*

Sales and Fear of Rejection

What is this all about?
All of this fear of non-acceptance.

Why do you care if they like you or not
Want to work with you or not
Approve of you or not?

It's uncomfortable to put yourself out there
When people say "No"
Yes, it's hard to hear
But avoiding fear gets you nowhere.

If they say "No," what's the worse that can happen?
Are you going to die?
Is the world going to end?

How much energy is being sucked out of you when you're
in avoidance?
How much weight is on your shoulders when you make
excuses

Procrastinate, and distract yourself from putting yourself out there?

Is this how you want to live...
Like a scaredy cat?

What do you want instead?

How can you step into the light
and shine bright?

Rejection from others is always a projection of where they're at.
It's never about you.
No need to take on their issues.

Put yourself out there.
Get used to the discomfort.
Step into your greatest possibilities.

Stop slamming the door on opportunities.
Fling your arms wide open to receive.

You will be amazed at the endless possibilities
When you face fear in the face and get out of your own way.

Heart Questions

How has fear of rejection and confrontation caused you to take on too much?
How has fear of not being liked by others caused you to take on too much?
Why is being liked so important to you?
Will you do anything to avoid uncomfortable situations and/or possible confrontations?
At what cost to your health, livelihood, and soul?
What are three risks you can take to get out of your comfort zone and put yourself out there to get what you want?
How do you want to feel about yourself and what can you do to create your desired feelings everyday?

Power Affirmations

I'm going to put my Big Girl panties on and put myself out there!

I'm getting over myself and stepping into my greatest possibilities.

It's ok if people say "no" because I'll still love me for me and I know the people meant for me will say, "Hell yes!"

Conversation Starters

How has fear of rejection been in the way of getting what you want?

How have you been in your own way and what are you going to do to get out of your way?

Does fear of rejection affect your sales? Do you want to break-free from fear of rejection and make more money? Visit www.Janna-Chin. com/Fear-of-Rejection for more Free tools.

Don't Take It Personally

"Don't take it personally. Nothing others do is because of you. What others say and do is a projection of their own reality. When you are immune to the opinion and actions of others, you won't be the victim of needless suffering." -Don Miguel Ruiz

Don't Take It Personally

When people break their promises and don't follow through
Don't take it personally.

When people say no
And don't value you or what you do
Don't take it personally.

When people don't show up
And flake out on you
Don't take it personally.

Why take on their insecurities, doubts, and lack of integrity?
Why make it about you when it's about them
And their inability be true.

If they break a promise, it's a reflection of them.

If they don't say yes to all that you have to offer, isn't it about them and what they think they need?

Why carry the burden of taking on their responsibilities? Save yourself some stress.

Don't take it personally...
You will feel so much more free, especially from your own judgments and insecurities.

Heart Questions

Do you ever take things personally in your work and relationships?

How does taking things personally affect your peace of mind, self-esteem, and confidence?

Have you ever lost time and energy worrying about what other people think about you?

Have you ever lost income because you took something personally?

What is your emotional trigger that always gets you feeling like it's personal and about you not being good enough?

How can you start to let go of your insecurities and stop taking things personally?

Power Affirmations

Nothing others do is about me.

What others do and say is a projection of their own reality.

Conversation Starters

Do you ever take things personally?

When do you always feel like it's personal even when it's probably not about you?

How can you stop judging yourself and others as not good enough when it feels personal?

The Day She Broke Up with Fear

"Most fears of rejection rest on the desire for approval from other people. Don't base your self-esteem on their opinions." -Harvey Mackay

The Day She Broke Up with Fear

That morning she awoke to the sound of mountain dew
She knew what she finally had to do.

She had to choose; choose between what she wanted
and what she knew.

Always torn between competing desires to be liked
and what she knew.

She risked it all.
All for the sake of survival.
She knew if she spoke her truth
She would get the beat down.

Anything to avoid the beat down
The abuse.
She could bear it no more.

There were only two roads for her to travel.
Keeping silent and suffering or
taking a stand for her livelihood.

But wait! Taking a stand meant confrontation.

Up until the day she awoke to the sound of mountain dew,
she had chosen survival
Fear was her constant companion.

That day she decided, decided to break up with fear and
stand for her livelihood, even if it meant confrontation
and rejection.

She did all this because she knew she could find a
better way,
that eventually would lead her to better days.

Heart Questions

Do you let other people's anger control you? If yes, explain. You can't control others, but what are some things you can do to take care of yourself when you're scared or when someone is trying to control you with their anger?
How has fear of rejection caused you to take on too much and what can you do to stand up for yourself?

Power Affirmations

I forgive myself for being stuck in fear.
I will honor my truth even when I fear confrontation and rejection.
I am confident and take risks to go after what I want.
I am free of fear of rejection and confrontation.
I am a lovable and worthwhile person.

Conversation Starters

Has fear of not being liked caused you to people please?

How have you avoided confrontation for fear of people's anger?

What can you do to better honor your thoughts and feelings?

Do you fear confrontation and rejection? Does your fear of rejection stop you from speaking your truth and standing up for yourself? Visit www.Janna-Chin.com/Fear-of-Rejection for more free tools.

There's Never Enough Money

There's Never Enough Money

There's never enough
never enough
it's kinda tough, tough when there's not enough.

So conditioned to believe this untruth
When all around us is abundance, everywhere we look-
there is so much that we can touch and use.
Enjoyment at our fingertips everything is taken care of
Even when we worry it doesn't change the story.

We still have no peace.
Serenity eludes us.
Possibilities gone
Because of the lack in ourselves, in our minds.

We make up the worry
It's not even our story.
We carry around the voices of other people's fear
Conditioned in us through the years.

We hear the voices, "You're poor."

We believe this in our core.
This is our poverty thinking that
We hold onto
No matter how untrue.

Reality isn't our focus.
We believe the hocus pocus.

"I don't have this and I don't have that."
What if it's all quack?

What if we're abundant as we are?
We can reach for the stars.
Move our reality so, so far... when we believe there's enough.
Always enough.
Wherever we are.

Heart Questions

How has scarcity thinking (thinking and believing that there's never enough money) created your reality of financial struggle and the reality of never having enough? Where did you learn that there's never enough?

How did your parents, authority figures, and culture reinforce your belief that there's never enough?

How has the belief of "never having enough" been reinforced by your thoughts and behaviors?

How do you give more and more power to the belief that you never have enough in your everyday thoughts and behaviors with money?

How often have you inadvertently reinforced this money myth by saying, "I can't afford it" and "There's never enough money to pay the bills?"

How has believing that there's never enough money affected your current situation with money?

What can you start to do to start shifting your money mindset from scarcity thinking to abundance thinking?

How can you empower your thoughts and behaviors to create a new reality of ease and financial abundance?

Power Affirmations

I always have more than enough of everything I need.
I have more money than I can ever spend in a lifetime.

Conversation Starters

Do you believe there's never enough?

Has your belief that there's never enough helped you to attract more ease and financial abundance into your life?

How can you start seeing and appreciating the abundance in your life more?

Do you want to clear your money blocks and receive more money? Do you want to shift your money mindset to manifest financial abundance? Visit **www.Janna-Chin.com/money** for a Free Women and Wealth Webinar and mp3.

In this webinar you will learn:

- The 3 Money Personalities
- The 5 money myths that may be silently sabotaging your wealth *and*
- How to improve your relationship with money!

Love Hate Relationship with Money

Love Hate Relationship with Money

I want you.
No I don't.

I need you.
You're greedy.

I just want to serve and make a difference.
You're selfish for wanting money.

There are people starving in the world.
You want more than you need.
Why are you so greedy?

I'm not doing it for the money.

You should be ashamed
for only thinking about yourself.

You don't really help
when all you're doing is
thinking about yourself.

"I'm not doing it for the money,"
You keep telling yourself.
Like a broken record, you really want it to be heard.
Somehow, if you convince yourself of these lies
You won't have to explain why…

You want more money.

Love. Hate.
I want you.
No, I don't.

Bills pile up.
Dreams lost.
Adventures you never take.

Push.
Pull.

"Money, I want you,
won't you please stay?"

Yes, if only you commit to wanting more money
coming your way without any shame.

Money Myths

Money myths are subconscious beliefs about money that *block* you from having more money and financial freedom.

As I share the following money myths, think about which money myths you've bought into and how they've affected your thoughts, feelings, behaviors, and relationship with money.

Money Myth #1

**The scarcity thinking money mindset is the mindset of limiting thoughts and *beliefs about money.* *It's the belief* that there's never enough money.

Scarcity thinking comes from adages we grew up hearing such as, "Money doesn't grow on trees."

As we become adults with more responsibilities and bills to pay, we continue to reinforce these thoughts and beliefs by often repeating, *"I can't afford it"* and *"There's never enough" when we want to buy something, but don't feel we can afford it.*

When we over-focus on scarcity thinking and limiting beliefs about money, it becomes our reality. We inadvertently create a self-fulfilling prophecy around money. If we believe we can't afford it and there's never enough, we really won't be able to afford it and will never have enough money.

Money Myth #2

Money will turn a good person into a bad person. This is an unconscious fear you may have cultivated from seeing people you know change when they became wealthy; they were once "good" people who turned "bad" because of their new-found wealth. The fear with this money mindset for many people is, "I don't want to turn into a bad person" so there is an unconscious rejection of money and anything related to financial prosperity including: work promotions, business and career success and monetary recognition.

This money myth has also been taught to us as a form of truth from the proverb, "Money is the root of all evil." If we believe that "Money is the root of all evil" and associate money as being bad, evil or dirty, we certainly don't want to have an abundance of it! We will unconsciously reject and shun money because we don't want to think of ourselves and others to perceive us as bad or evil.

In order for you to manifest more money and end the emotional roller coaster with money, you will need to break-free from these money myths and learn practical tools to manage and grow your money.

Do you want to improve your relationship with money? Do you want financial freedom? Visit www.Janna-Chin.com/Money for a free women and wealth webinar and mp3. In this webinar you will learn:

- The five money myths that may be silently sabotaging your wealth *and*
- How to improve your relationship with money!

Money Grows on Trees

*"There is nothing more spiritual than prosperity,
because prosperity is the touching, feeling,
tasting of alignment." -Abraham Hicks*

Money Grows on Trees

Money is what you see.
It's not all that it's cut out to be.
Money is what you need, but does not define your reality.
It's what's in your heart that matters most.
Money is just energy used for trade, to buy things that we need.
It's not good or bad. But we think it is.
We judge ourselves for wanting and secretly yearning for it;
Yet, we tell ourselves it's wrong and judge our wanting of it as greed- somehow impure when it's just paper that really does grow from trees.

Demystify the yearning for money as bad and impure and see it for what it is
something that can make our lives joyous and free!

Embrace money.
Reach for money.
Open your arms to money
and it will come to you in droves.

Stop running from it like it's bad
Don't chastise yourself for wanting it and then

Lie to yourself, "It's not about the money"
Allowing condemnation to seep in for wanting what you
feel, deep down, you shouldn't have.

Money will set you free when you allow it to be part of
your reality.
Money can create happiness or whatever you choose it
to be.

Heart Questions

Where have you bought into the idea that money is bad?
Growing up, did you hear the phrase, "Money is the root of all evil?"
What does, "Money is the root of all evil" mean to you?
How does this belief affect your relationship with money?
How has this belief affected your openness to receiving more money?
How does this belief affect your decisions and behaviors around money?
How has scarcity thinking and worrying about money affected your bank account balance?
Do you want just enough money to pay the bills or do you want to have an abundance of money so you will always be able to afford necessities and everything you want?
What are your beliefs about money?
How does your money mindset and beliefs about money block you from manifesting more financial abundance into your life?
Do you want to be rich? Why or why not?
Does your body cringe (or constrict) at the thought of wanting to be rich?
Why is there a negative connotation with being rich?
Have you ever been shamed for wanting money and things money could buy?
Where does the shame and guilt about wanting money come from?
How will you afford to have the experiences you want without an abundance of money?
Is it possible to be a good person and still want more money and want to be rich?

If you were rich and had all the money you ever needed, what kind of person would you be?

Would you let money change you?

How would you spend your money?

Are you willing to receive more money?

What can you do to be more receptive to receiving financial abundance and wealth?

What money mindset will you need to *allow* more financial abundance into your life?

What money habits will you will need to change to better manage your money and create financial wealth?

Power Affirmations

Money does come from trees and I can be as abundant as I want to be.

Money is everywhere. All I have to do is ask the Universe, believe, and be ready to receive.

Conversation Starters

Growing up, did you hear the saying, "Money doesn't grow on trees?"

How did that experience affect you, your relationship with money, and your openness to receive more abundance?

Do you want to learn powerful tools to grow your money? Do you want to create financial freedom? Visit www.Janna-Chin.com/money for free Women and Wealth Webinars and mp3s. In these webinars, you will learn:

- What a healthy relationship with money looks like
- How to create your money vision for daily inspiration
- How to shift your feelings from stress and not enough to appreciation and celebration every time you make a purchase!

Miracles

"Today I welcome infinite possibilities. With open arms I accept the support of the Universe. I know that creative abundance is available to me now. I expect miracles." -Gabrielle Bernstein

Miracles

Believing in the unseen
The unknown

A deep belief and knowing
That all is well
And what you truly desire will be shown

It will appear
When you least expect it
As long as you're clear about what you want

Take action
Dream it
Desire it
Feel it
Believe your wishes will come true
No matter how crazy or deluded it may seem
Believe in all possibilities

Have faith in the unknown
And in time
It will all be shown
Manifested miracles
Yours to call your own

Heart Questions

How often do you practice faith, the belief in the unseen and unknown?

If you don't practice faith often, what gets in the way of your faith- your belief in great possibilities and manifested miracles?

Have there been times in your life when pleasant surprises i.e., times when situations worked out even when you were worried and stressed about the situation.

Identify three situations that worked out for you even though you didn't think it was possible.

Could any or all of those situations been considered miracles?

What can you do daily to strengthen your faith and belief in miracles?

When you're afraid of the unknown and uncertain about your future, how can you take shelter in God and trust in what you can't yet see?

How can you strengthen your faith and belief in possibilities?

What worries get in the way of your belief in the power of God, The Divine, and/or the Universe?

What are some positive-self-talk statements you could use to soothe your worries about the unknown and fears about the future?

The definition of a miracle is, "A shift in perception from fear to love."

-Marianne Williamson

During times of fear and worry, how can you shift your perception from fear to love?

What can you think, say, or do to make this shift in perception from fear to love real for you?
How can you see the person or situation through the eyes of love, rather than through fear and anxiety?

Love Intention Exercise

Write a love intention to shift your consciousness from fear and anxiety to love, trust, and faith in miracles. When you set an intention, you are defining an attitude, mindset, and a goal that you wish to become your reality.

Below is an example of a love intention that will help you transform fear and worry about money to love, trust and gratitude.

When I'm worried about money, I will cherish the money I do have. I will be grateful for the priceless riches in my life. I expect miracles. I trust and know that all will be taken care of today and everyday.

Love Intention Template

When I'm _____. I
will _____.

I expect _____. I trust
and know _____.

Power Affirmations

I expect miracles and know the Universe has already lined up my heart's desires.
My faith is so much stronger than my fears.

 **Conversation Starters**

Do you believe in miracles?

How would you describe your faith?

How could you strengthen your faith?

Share a time when you experienced a miracle or manifested your desires.

Love In The Air

Love In The Air

Love in the air
It is in the flair
of love in the air
that I feel this beautiful embrace
of self-acceptance.

Free from judgment
I'm able to let go of expectations
and let others be
who they want to be.

Best of all, I'm free to be me.

Embracing my beautiful spirit.
I'll soar to new heights
I've never before seen.

I'll experience the wonders of the world
Fresh and free.
Connect with the love and beauty inside of me and
Give it away to everyone I see… ever so freely.

Coming home to myself,
I dwell in this beautiful moment.
Cherishing the best version of me.

Always. Eternally.

The Beginning of a
New You

The Beginning of a New You

For over ten years, I've worked with women entrepreneurs from all over the country. During that time, I've discovered that no matter their upbringing or personal circumstances, smart women entrepreneurs share the same experiences of stress, anxiety, worry, and lack of confidence that leads to loss of: energy, peace of mind, health and vitality, financial opportunities, and wealth. The good news is that by shifting your mindset and using the right tools or working with a coach like myself, it is truly possible to get out of overwhelm and love yourself to wealth.

The key to success is for you to use the tools I've shared with you in this book. I promise, if you do the work, you will experience the results. I have had the wonderful honor and privilege of working with hundreds of clients that have experienced transformational, life-changing results using the tools I've shared with you. No matter how many times I've witnessed these life-changing miracles and have worked myself out of a job in just a few sessions, I always feel an incredible sense of joy when I see my clients go from completely hopeless and exhausted to vibrant, prosperous, and free! Words just can't describe the happiness I feel when I see my clients creating great value and contribution in the world and really making a difference--while loving themselves to wealth with ease and joy as the best version of themselves.

If you'd like to experience even deeper results, start an Overwhelmed *No More!* women's group and/or book club to create a sisterhood of support. Or, start a Meetup in your area using this book as a guide. By doing so, you would be "paying it forward," helping yourself deeply, and creating a community of support of like-minded women. Here you can experience heartfelt conversations, and true connection, without the stress and overwhelm.

I'm grateful to have had the experience of burning myself out so completely that I was bedridden and incapacitated from debilitating pain and exhaustion. Why? Learning from the depths of this life-changing experience of hopelessness and despair, I successfully healed and reinvented my life and career. I am now able to offer the tools I learned and created from my journey out of overwhelm, to loving myself to wealth, connecting and supporting the clients I personally work with and the coaches I certify through the Overwhelmed *No More!* Licensing Program.

My biggest hope for you is that you take the time to use the inspiration and tools I've shared in this book, so that you too, can experience the magic, ease, and joy of life without overwhelm. This truly can be a life filled with self-love, freedom, abundance, and wealth for you!

Overwhelmed *No More!* Love Yourself to Wealth Coaching Program

I'm pleased to present, The **Overwhelmed** *No More!* Love Yourself to Wealth Coaching Program. A program that powerfully supports women with breaking-free from being overwhelmed and creating more financial abundance in their lives. The program includes: both live and virtual personal and group coaching, masterminds, women and wealth, money mindset, and law of attraction trainings and workshops.

Janna also offers complimentary private sessions for women entrepreneurs ready to break-free from overwhelm and create the life and business they really want. Space is limited. If you're interested in learning more and receiving free Overwhelmed *No More!* Love Yourself to Wealth tools, visit www.Janna-Chin.com.

Overwhelmed *No More!*
Love Yourself to Wealth
Licensing Program

Are you a change-maker and naturally a good listener?

Do you want to be part of a movement that's transforming lives and helping women be the best version of themselves while making a big difference on the planet?

If you answered yes to any of the above, visit www. Janna-Chin.com/licensing to discover how you can be an Overwhelmed *No More!* Love Yourself to Wealth Coach.

Invite Janna to Speak at Your Event

Janna loves to connect with her audience. Whether it's a group of leaders, high-achieving entrepreneurs or a room filled with college students, she will empower and inspire you with her energy and charm. Janna is available to speak at universities, conferences, and business events.

Visit www.Janna-Chin.com/speaking to learn more and to book Janna to speak at your event.

About the Author

Janna Chin, MA is a Life and Business Coach. She is known as the 'Burnout Slayer' and 'Profit Accelerator' with a track record for working herself out of a job in just a few sessions. Janna is a transformational coach and educator with over a decade of coaching and teaching experience. She is the founder of the **Overwhelmed** *No More!* Love Yourself to Wealth Coaching Program that inspires women to powerfully break-free from being overwhelmed and overcome the guilt and expectations of being 'Superwomen' in a culture that fosters near perfection. Janna loves to empower women to break-free from patterns and fears that no longer serve them. She is truly passionate about inspiring women to fully embrace life without overwhelm so that they can be the best version of themselves and make a bigger difference. Janna provides the tools and roadmap for women to actualize their dreams; to play all out and fully live— with more ease, joy and financial abundance!

www.ingramcontent.com/pod-product-compliance
Lightning Source LLC
Chambersburg PA
CBHW020736180526
45163CB00001B/256